CURIOUS CAMI LEARNS ABOUT FAMILIES

AUTHOR: AMELIA LEEKS
CO-AUTHOR: CAMILLE BELLAMY

Curious Cami Learns About Families
Copyright 2020 by Amelia Leeks and Camille Bellamy. All rights reserved.

No part of this publication may be reproduced, stored in a retrieval system, or transmitted in any way, by any means, whether electronically, mechanically, via photocopy, recording, or otherwise without the prior written permission of the publisher except as provided by USA copyright law.

Published by TJS Publishing House
www.tjspublishinghouse.com
IG: @ tjspublishinghouse
FB: @ tjspublishinghouse
tjspublishinghouse@gmail.com

Published in the United States of America
ISBN-13: 978-1-952833-09-0
ISBN-10: 1-952833-09-4

DEDICATION

This book is dedicated to my one and only girl, Cami. Everything I have ever learned about love has come from raising you. I am a product of a single-family home, as are you, but the two of us are destined for greatness. We have the greatest father of all time, God. I thank God every day for choosing me to be your mom. As you grow, continue to be curious, ask many questions. Dream really big, and explore this world.

ACKNOWLEDGMENTS

First and foremost, we would like to thank God Almighty for giving us the strength and inspiration to write this book. We would like to thank our family and friends who have supported us throughout the years. We are blessed to have a village that prays for us. So many people have been with us on this journey called life, and we are grateful for your continuous love & support.

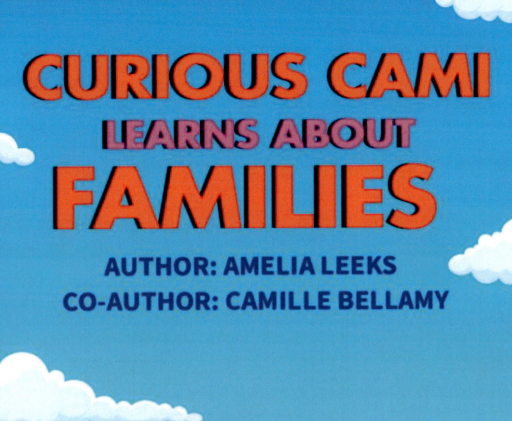

CURIOUS CAMI
LEARNS ABOUT
FAMILIES

AUTHOR: AMELIA LEEKS
CO-AUTHOR: CAMILLE BELLAMY

Who would have ever guessed there would be a girl with so much curiosity? Cami is so curious! She always asks lots and lots of questions. She asks this, and she asks that, but her mom always finds a way to answer her.

One day, while heading to the library, she asked her mom, "What is a family?"

Her mom said, "Cami, a family is a group of people that love one another."

Cami said, "But mom, it's four people in my friend Gabby's family. A mom, a dad, Gabby, and her baby brother."

Her mom said, Cami, families come in many different sizes, shapes, and colors."

"Why is it just the two of us?"

Her mom was stunned but knew she had to respond. So she said, "Cami let's go to the library and learn about families."

Her mom picked up a book about families and began to read it to curious Cami. The story was about the differences in families. It was a story her mom read a long time ago, and she knew it would come in handy.

"Some families are big, and some are small," Cami's mom read.

"Some families are short, and some are tall."

"Some families are slender, and some are round."

"Some families are yellow, and some are brown."

"Some families are young; some are old."

"Some families are shy, and some are bold."

"Some families are happy, and some are sad."

"Some families stay calm, and some get really mad."

"Some families are here, and some are there, some families are everywhere."

"Cami, we are all different in every kind of way. Just remember family will love each other no matter where they stay."

Cami said, "Mom, I understand no one is the same. It can be two or three, but family is love like you and me."

ABOUT THE AUTHOR

Amelia Leeks is a single mom who was inspired to write books for single-parent homes. She is from Newark, NJ, and attended South Carolina State University for her undergraduate education. Amelia enjoys educating the youth. She has created multiple platforms for affirming young girls, such as Pretty Little Visionaries, Charming to Be Me, & Fix My Crown. She has been a troop leader for Girl Scouts for six years. Amelia is a member of Delta Sigma Theta Sorority, Inc.

The co-author, Camille Bellamy (Cami), is Amelia's daughter. Camille is the inspiration behind this book. Cami wanted to understand why her family was just a mom and herself. Cami is a kind-hearted ten-year-old who enjoys playing games with her friends, singing, and dancing. Cami has been a Girl Scout for six years. This mother-daughter duo wants all children of single-parent homes to understand that they are special too.

Want to learn more about Amelia and Cami? Do so by visiting their website, www.sheopensuplife.com.

Made in the USA
Columbia, SC
16 November 2020